I SPY

GOLD
CHALLENGER!

A BOOK OF
PICTURE
RIDDLES

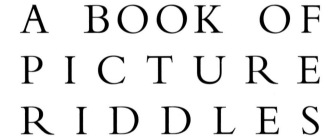

Photographs by Walter Wick

Riddles by Jean Marzollo

Cartwheel
·B·O·O·K·S·®

SCHOLASTIC INC.
New York Toronto London Auckland Sydney
Mexico City New Delhi Hong Kong Buenos Aires

For my mother

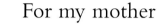

W.W.

For Clorae Evereteze Prince Diaz

J.M.

Book design by Carol Devine Carson

Go to www.scholastic.com for Web site information
on Scholastic authors and illustrators.

Library of Congress Cataloging-in-Publication Data

Wick, Walter.
    I spy gold challenger!: a book of picture riddles / photographs by Walter Wick; riddles
by Jean Marzollo.
        p.   cm. — (I spy books)
    Summary: Rhyming text leads the reader to find objects hidden in the photographs.
    ISBN 0-590-04296-3
    1. Picture puzzles—Juvenile literature.   2. Riddles
    [1. Picture puzzles.]   I. Marzollo, Jean.   II. Title.   III. Series
    GV1507.P47W5295   1998
    793.735—dc21   98-13982
                                                                                                    CIP
                                                                                                    AC
25 24 23 22 21   05 06 07

Printed in Mexico   49
First printing, September 1998

TABLE OF CONTENTS

Picture riddles fill this book;
Turn the pages! Take a look!

Use your mind, use your eye;
Read the riddles — play I SPY!

I spy a turtle, four ladders, and SAND,
Three baseball gloves, and a picture of land;

Four birdies of blue, nine bowling pins,
A balloon, a mask, and two swim fins.

I spy a heart, a starfish, a frog,

A towel, a trowel, a taxi, a dog;

Seven horses, a barrel, a duck that is teeny,
Two real feathers, and a surfer's bikini.

I spy a lamb, a candle, a van,

An old shoelace, and a potbellied man;

A baby bottle, a fancy shoe,
Two paper houses, and two giraffes, too.

13

I spy a spool, seven arrows, a veil,

A stop light, a meter, a small sack of mail;

An alligator car, a standing clothespin,
Fifty-six people, plus a happy grin.

I spy three musical instruments to play,
Two matches, a dog, a trunk, and a tray;

A triangle button, a small metal nail,
The shadow of a bat, and a lion's tail.

I spy a screw, a skateboard, a spring,
A turkey, a bottle, an elastic string;

18

REINDEER, RAILROAD, three smokestacks, a clock,
An ear with eyes, and a little blue sock.

I spy a ruler, a fan, two D's,

A puzzle piece, a bike, two V's;

Three ants, a giraffe, a green reptile,
A shoelace, a saw, and a bearded smile.

I spy a dustpan, a shutter, a cork,
Antlers, a drill bit, a boy, and a fork;

A feather, a wrench, two telephone poles,
A sewing machine, and a brick with holes.

I spy a hydrant, a platter, a 3,
A chain, a car, a kettle for tea;

A bottle cap, a thimble spring,
Three silver straws, and a feathery wing.

I spy a sailboat, a ruler, a D,

A polka-dot sock, four cats, and TEA;

Five paper clips, and a panda bear,
And two white birds that aren't really there.

I spy an acorn, an upside-down STAR,

Goggles, suspenders, a red race car;

Two white beards, a moon, a lock,
Six bears, seven hats, and a snowy sock.

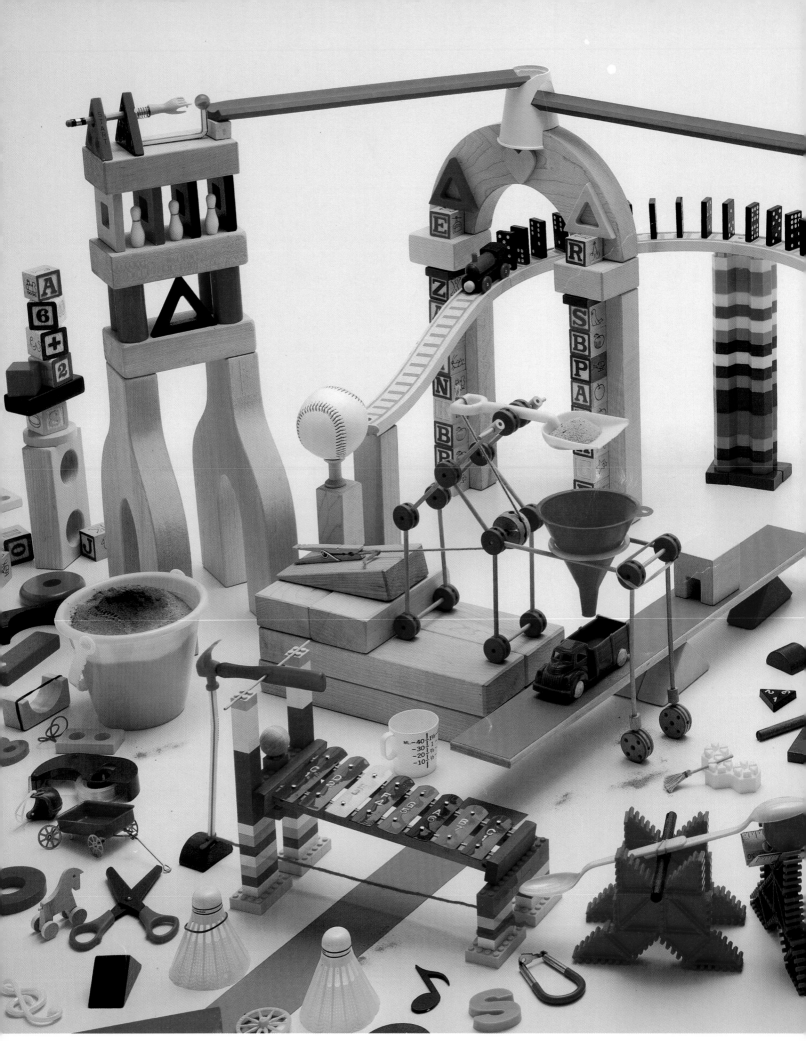

I spy two pencils, and a porcupine,
Two cups, a nut, and a double nine;

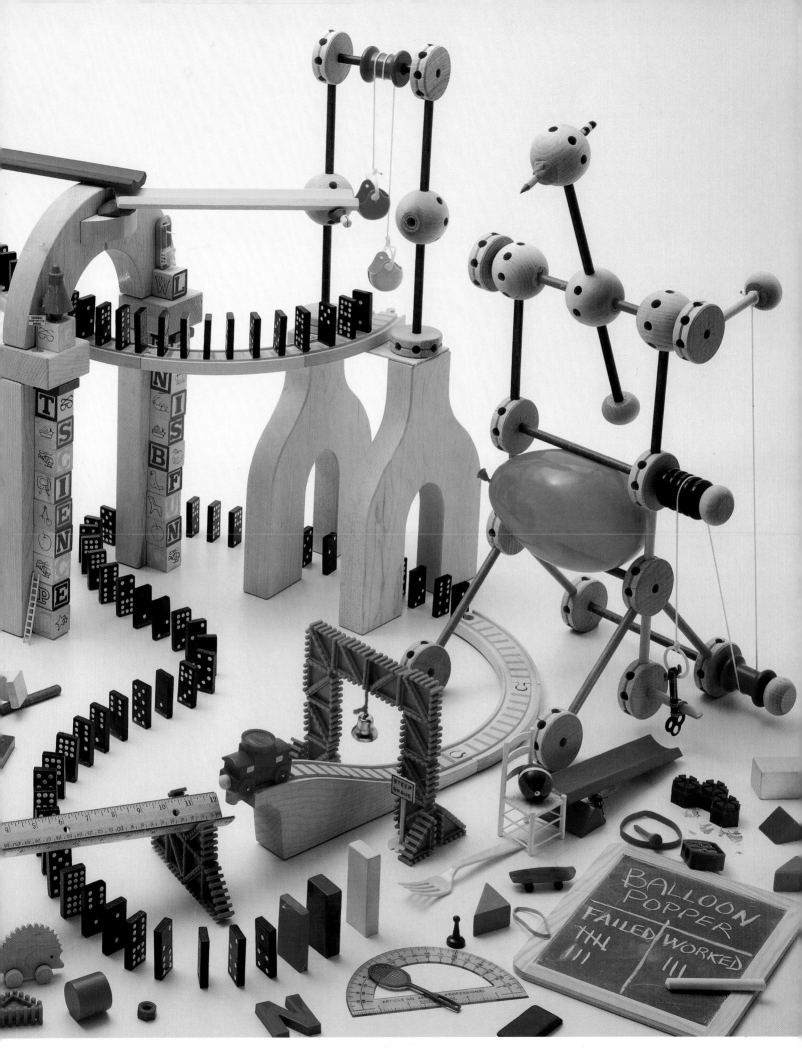

Two straws, wood shavings on the floor,
And something that's also on page 24.

EXTRA CREDIT RIDDLES

Find the Pictures That Go With These Riddles:

I spy a dog, a tight yellow knot,

A yellow boot, and something that's hot.

I spy a marble that's red and white,

Two googly eyes, a gear, and a knight.

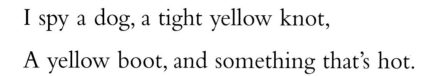

I spy a swan, a red-and-yellow flower,

A spool, a drum, and a little white tower.

I spy two arrows, a domino, a chain,

Two hot bones, and a horse's mane.

I spy a seashell, toe prints, a tree,

A guy with no shirt, and a ship at sea.

I spy a peanut, a small rolling pin,

Two horses, a broom, and a dorsal fin.

I spy a broom, a fork, a TV,

A vertical boat, and a little golf tee.

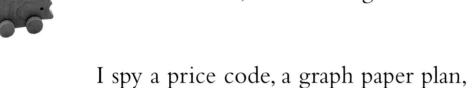

I spy a price code, a graph paper plan,

A hungry blue ape, and a briefcase man.

I spy a nutcracker, a magnet man,

Three T's, a B, and a frying pan.

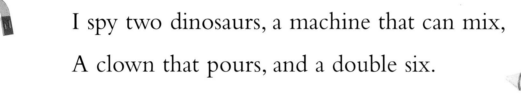

I spy two dinosaurs, a machine that can mix,

A clown that pours, and a double six.

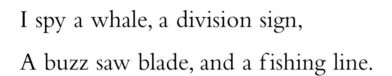

I spy a whale, a division sign,

A buzz saw blade, and a fishing line.

I spy a stroller, clock hands, and GO,

MILK'S THE ONE, a hydrant, and SLOW.